Original title:
The Door that Opens

Copyright © 2025 Creative Arts Management OÜ
All rights reserved.

Author: Harris Montgomery
ISBN HARDBACK: 978-1-80587-079-1
ISBN PAPERBACK: 978-1-80587-549-9

Beyond the Barrier

There's a wall that I can't climb,
But I heard it's just a mime.
I asked it for the secret key,
It laughed and said, 'Just follow me!'

I tippy-toed and tried to peek,
But all I saw was a cheeky streak.
A squirrel in a tiny hat,
Yelled, 'Run fast, you silly cat!'

Unlocking Hidden Potential

I found a box, it looked quite stout,
With clues inside, or so I thought.
When I turned the rusty lock,
Out popped a chicken — what a shock!

It clucked a tune, I joined the dance,
A cha-cha with a feathered chance.
Potential lost in fowl delight,
We laughed until we saw the light!

Threshold of the Imagination

I stood before a colorful gate,
Wondering what could await.
With a wiggle and a silly grin,
I tiptoed back — let the fun begin!

A giant gnome proclaimed with glee,
'You'll need a hat to ride the spree!'
I grabbed a rainbow from the air,
And off we went without a care!

The Latch on Tomorrow

Tomorrow's latch is hard to find,
It hides behind ideas, unrefined.
With a giggle, I knocked once more,
To see what gadgets it had in store!

A roller skate, a flying seal,
A pogo stick that made me squeal.
I bounced right into future's plan,
And so I hopped — a magic man!

Threshold to Possibility

When I stumbled on this mat,
A cat sat down, quite like a brat.
It laughed at me, with all its might,
As I tripped and took flight.

Each step I take leads to a scene,
With clowns and pies, it's all quite keen.
I wear a hat that's far too tall,
And juggle dreams, I might just fall.

The sill has jokes, of every kind,
It whispers secrets, never maligned.
A peek reveals a dance charade,
Where socks and shoes have plans displayed.

What lies beyond this twisted grin?
A land where laughter surely wins.
I'll hop and skip to worlds anew,
With laughter loud, and joy in view.

Passageway to Dreams

In a hall of socks, one left behind,
A portal opens; it's quite unrefined.
There's a parade of ducks with flair,
And dancing spoons—Oh, what a pair!

I tiptoe on marshmallows sweet,
As unicorns prance on unlikely feet.
Each corner I round brings giggles galore,
As candy canes sprout from the floor.

The ceiling sings in a falsetto tone,
While jellybeans start to play alone.
A trampoline bounces on clouds of cream,
In this place, reality's just a meme.

With wild creatures that twist and twine,
Twirling and whirling, all divine.
This journey leads to laughter's embrace,
Where dreams unfold with a silly grace.

Gateway of Unwritten Journeys

Through a crack in the wall, I spy a scene,
With unicorns sipping from a soda machine.
They wave their hooves and offer a sip,
As I tumble in on an upside-down trip.

The carpet's a river where fish wear hats,
Swinging their tails like circus acrobats.
A giraffe gives a wink, and oh so sly,
"In this world, you can always fly!"

Above, a chandelier made of jam,
Swings gently while singing a tune of spam.
Each step on the floor brings giggles and sighs,
As sneakers sprout wings to my surprise.

Let's journey through puzzles and riddles galore,
With treasure chests filled with snacks to explore.
Unwritten paths just waiting to start,
With every twist, we leap and we dart.

Veil of New Horizons

A curtain sways, with polka dot cheer,
Behind it, a land where snacks appear.
Please, take a seat on a bubblegum cloud,
Where laughter rings out, boisterous and loud.

Dancing muffins in a conga line,
Offer me slices of pizza divine.
With each twirl, the world's in a spin,
A rollercoaster ride where the fun begins.

I meet a wise owl who's lost his glasses,
Who tells me stories of wacky masses.
Kites that take off with a belly laugh,
Create a dance on this hilarious path.

So, I step through this veil of delight,
Where cookies fall like stars at night.
Adventure awaits past giggles and grins,
In this crazy place, let the fun begin!

The Whispering Arch

In the corner of my room, it stands,
Chattering secrets like a set of bands.
It rattles and giggles, shoelaces untied,
Maybe it's just a cheeky slide.

A glimpse of the kitchen, it's pleading for pie,
To steal a hot snack, oh me, oh my!
Yet here I am, just a curious chap,
Listening to whispers, caught in the flap.

One day it sighed, "Please, don't walk by!"
But who would believe a door can cry?
So I'll sit and I'll giggle at its silly behest,
A chatty old frame, quite the jest!

The Key of Revelation

Stumbling upon a key, rusty and bent,
What could it unlock? I wondered, quite intent.
A treasure of cookies or perhaps just a book,
Mysterious mysteries—oh, it's worth a look!

Twirling it 'round, in the keyhole it went,
The door creaked open with a humorous dent.
Instead of a castle, with knights in a joust,
Out popped a squirrel, just as I passed!

"Fancy a nibble?" he asked with a wink,
"Just don't tell the cat, he's not one to blink."
So I laughed with a nutty friend by my side,
This journey revealed, what a wild ride!

Gateway to Shadows

In shadows it lingered, a mischief-filled gate,
Promising giggles, perhaps a new fate.
I pushed it with glee, whisked into the night,
Only to tumble into a pile of bright light!

Yet instead of darkness and goblins quite grim,
There were puppies and kittens, oh what a whim!
They danced all around, in a comical spin,
Making shadows chuckle as their day did begin.

"Come join our party!" they yapped with delight,
Card games and laughter, oh what a sight!
So I seized the adventure, with joy on my face,
Turns out the shadows were a hilarious place!

Entry into New Realities

A rickety frame with a sign that just reads,
'Enter if you dare, bring snacks and some seeds!'
Curiosity struck, so I gave it a push,
In I went, feeling quite the full mush.

I stepped into worlds with spaghetti-topped hats,
And dancing in slippers with chorus of cats.
They juggled my worries, made silly balloon,
In this wacky realm, I felt like a loon!

With a cheer and a laugh, they threw me a pie,
I dodged and I dived, oh me, oh my!
From this day forth, I'd always recall,
Life's better with laughter when we answer the call!

Pathway to Tomorrow

In a pair of shoes that squeak,
I dance down paths, quite unique.
With a hop and a skip, I sway,
On this funny road, I play.

Every step brings a surprise,
Like a pie in the face, oh my!
Laughter echoes as I trip,
On this journey, I won't skip.

Clowns juggle dreams and sights,
Under the glow of marquee lights.
With each twist, I take a chance,
Inviting joy with every glance.

So here I stand, ready to leap,
Into tomorrows, wide and deep.
With a wink and a silly grin,
Let the adventures now begin!

Ripple of New Discoveries

Splash of giggles in the air,
With each splash, there's joy to spare.
Bouncing off the banks of fate,
Every ripple does await.

Canoes full of laughter row,
Down the stream where sillies flow.
Unexpected turns in tow,
What next, I do not know!

With a map drawn by crayons bright,
Swirling colors, pure delight.
Chasing shadows, racing light,
This discovery feels so right.

So paddle on, don't hesitate,
Adventure calls, we're never late.
With each funny twist and turn,
More to learn and hearts will burn!

The Lingering Entrance

A sign that winks and beckons me,
This entrance holds a mystery.
It squeaks and groans with every touch,
And giggles, oh, it loves too much!

A shadow of a dancing hat,
Says, "Come on in, and don't be flat!"
Cracking jokes and silly rhymes,
This place is just a ball of climes.

Doorknobs spin like tops in flight,
Each twist uncovers pure delight.
With every step, the humor swells,
In corners where the laughter dwells.

So make your choice, don't drag your feet,
Inside awaits a funny treat.
Adventures linger, bright and bold,
Come take a peek, let stories unfold!

The Searing Invitation

A fanfare of bright balloons,
And wacky hats that sing off tunes.
This is a feast, come grab a plate,
Not for the shy, but for those who create.

With scented candles lit just so,
They flicker as the giggles grow.
A table full of joy and cheer,
For all who dare to persevere.

Pin the tail on the moonlit night,
Where silly games take joyous flight.
Every bite brings a teasing grin,
It's a warm hug where laughs begin.

So step right up and take a chance,
In this invitation, let's all dance.
With food and friends in wild array,
Life's a carnival, come out and play!

Frame of Fresh Horizons

A frame hangs crooked on the wall,
It leads to nowhere, or so we call.
But when we peek and take a glance,
We find ourselves in a silly dance.

The world outside is bright and bold,
With talking cats and tales retold.
A rainbow horse trots by with glee,
Inviting us to join, with tea!

We skip through puddles made of juice,
And slide on cookies, oh what a truce!
The breeze smells of pop and cotton candy,
Who knew horizons could feel so dandy?

So here we stand, in giggles caught,
With every silly thought we sought.
Just frame the moment, hold it near,
We laugh so hard, we shed a tear!

Gateway to Whispers Beyond

A rusted gate creaks with a wink,
It promises secrets, or so we think.
We tiptoe close, with minds so hazy,
What lies beyond? Could it be crazy?

With each whisper, a voice like cheese,
Telling tales of squirrels and breeze.
A lizard in glasses reads from a book,
We stop and stare, oh, come take a look!

The ground is made of jelly, so sweet,
We bounce around like it's a treat.
Giggling goblins join the affair,
Creating stories beyond compare.

So open the gate, let's take the plunge,
In this world, there's room to grunge.
We giggle and joke as we dream along,
In whispers and laughter, we all belong!

Windows to the Unknown

A window cracked with curtains old,
Peering in, we find tales untold.
A sandwich sings in a jazzy tone,
While socks in pairs have a party alone!

The sun winks in, with a mischievous glow,
Painting the floor in a lively show.
Dancing shadows that shuffle and sway,
Invite us to join, let's laugh and play!

A teapot thinks it's a grand duke,
While curtains gossip, oh what a fluke!
Each smile and giggle spins a new thread,
In this odd world where nonsense is spread.

So press your nose against the glass,
Let the peculiar in, don't let it pass.
Glorious whimsy awaits our approach,
In windows where we joyfully broach!

The Key to Transformations

A key with sparkles, oh, what could it do?
Unlock mysteries, or maybe askew.
We twist it around, hoping for fun,
What if we turn into a bun?

With a click and a clack, we're shaped like pies,
Flying squirrels, oh, look at the skies!
We giggle at transforms so absurd,
A pizza slice speaks, 'Aren't I heard?'

Now we're balloons rising with flair,
Tickling clouds as we float in the air.
With every flip, we laugh till we cry,
In this mad world where only dreams fly!

So find the key, let's crank it loud,
In the land of the silly, we'll stand proud.
Transform and tumble, let whims take reign,
In the joyful chaos, we'll never feel plain!

Crossing Into New Chapters

With a nudge and a push, I go,
Into pages unraveled, a grand show.
My cat thinks it's all a game,
Chasing shadows, oh what a claim.

Doodles and scribbles, my mind's delight,
Each turn of the page feels just right.
A slip on the cover, oops, look at me,
Falling through laughter, so wild and free.

New tales await, with giggles galore,
Each chapter's a party, who could want more?
With every mishap and joyous mistake,
I dance through the words, delightful earthquake.

So here I am, with a grin on my face,
Turned over to whimsy, a colorful place.
Where blunders are treasures, and fun is the plan,
Crossing new chapters, I'm my own biggest fan.

Gateway of Altered Paths

I stumbled upon this strange portal, oh dear,
Where squirrels hold meetings, sipping on beer.
They gossip about nuts, their daily routine,
While I stand amazed, like a lost tambourine.

A sign overhead reads, 'No shoes allowed!',
It's a wacky new world, I'm laughing out loud.
Upside-down trees and clouds that wear hats,
Dancing with hedgehogs, and chatting with rats.

What's that over there? A whale on a bike!
Riding through puddles and zooming on spikes.
He calls out my name, offers a ride,
"Hop on, my friend, let's take a wild slide!"

Each twist brings a chuckle, a one-liner cheer,
I'm flung into laughter, let go of my fear.
In this gateway of paths, where silliness reigns,
I'm lost in the joy, it's where fun remains.

Transitioning Through Shadow

In the corner, a shadow seems to dance,
With twirls and jiggles, it took a chance.
"Hey there, do you mind if I take the lead?"
It shimmies and giggles, growing wild with speed.

A tap on the back, "You're welcome, my friend,"
As I trip and stumble—will this ever end?
It's a slippery slide, into daylight now,
With shadows that holler, "No worries, just wow!"

I tried to keep steady, but who would have guessed,
That every misstep is really a jest?
We leap through the corners, I laugh all the way,
In this shadowy world, it's a comical play.

With a wink and a nod, the shadows depart,
Leaving me smiling, a bounce in my heart.
Transition complete, from darkness to cheer,
I'll dance with the shadows anytime they're near.

Frame of Unexpected Encounters

I walked through a frame, felt a strange little tug,
Upon stepping inside, I met a talking bug.
"Have you seen my hat? It's quite a fine thing,"
He buzzed with a flair, as he started to sing.

In this unusual realm, where quirks play their part,
A three-legged dog played chess with an art.
"Checkmate!" it barked, with a wag of its tail,
I laughed at the scene, not a thing could derail.

Elves in bright costumes, with shoes made of cheese,
Shoulder to shoulder, they danced with such ease.
This frame of encounters is bursting with glee,
Where laughter's an anthem, and weird is the key.

So snap up the moments in bizarre frames of bliss,
For here lies the magic, the smile, the kiss.
With each twist and turn, let the fun be profound,
In this wild, quirky world, joy knows no bounds.

The Unsung Threshold

There's a frame that creaks with glee,
Keeps teasing what might be.
An old cat strolls right by,
Dreaming of a fishy pie.

Knobs that jiggle in a dance,
A squirrel sneaks a tiny glance.
With each squeak, a laugh we find,
What secrets lurk? Oh, never mind!

Shoes untied, a hat askew,
Will this lead to something new?
Each step brings a chuckle loud,
The threshold's antics, quite the crowd!

As we tip-toe on the brink,
Could it all just be a wink?
We giggle, stumble, slice the air,
What awaits? A bear? Or just a chair?

Frame of Untold Stories

A frame hangs crooked on the wall,
Is it art? Or just a brawl?
It whispers tales of wedgie fights,
And sock wars in the moonlit nights.

Peeking at the world so sly,
It always says a slight goodbye.
The cat jumps in, and oh dear me,
It's caught in yarn—what a sight to see!

Behind each wood, a giggle waits,
A tale of socks and petty fates.
The shadows dance with goofy flair,
While secrets barge in, unaware.

The stories bound to make us grin,
Chasing shadows under our skin.
A frame, a laugh, a playful jest,
Each glance reveals a new quest!

Key to Present Possibilities

With a twist of something bright,
The key unlocks, oh what a sight!
But wait, what's this? A pickle jar,
Staring back—my, how bizarre!

Each turn brings a bubbling laugh,
A shoe and sock, a broken staff.
What's behind? A dancing moose?
In this world, there's no excuse!

The key falls short, it stumbles too,
As we turn, the plot does skew.
A chorus sings—flashing lights!
Inside, we find the weirdest sights.

So twist away, don't hesitate,
What's next in our twist of fate?
Each sound a chuckle, each laugh a cheer,
Possibilities hide everywhere here!

The Hushed Invitation

A note slips through with a quiet cue,
It says, 'Join me for a hullabaloo!'
Peeking under the big brown mat,
Is it a party, or just a cat?

The whispers float like ticklish air,
An invitation, a secret to share.
Shhh! The cupcakes start to dance,
While jellybeans take a prance!

Every step feels like a game,
Will I win, or is it lame?
The hush grows loud with giggly leaps,
As fantastical chaos peeks!

So bring your whimsy, don't delay,
The hush invites, let's join the play.
With laughter swirling in the air,
Who knows? It's wild, it's beyond compare!

Gateway to Tomorrow's Embrace

In the hall of shoes that squeak,
My cat thinks it's a peak.
She jumps to see what's ahead,
Only to find the neighbor's shed.

With a wiggle and a shake,
She thinks it's hers to take.
In this game of hide and seek,
Tomorrow's surprises look so cheek!

On the brink of great delight,
A toaster gives a fright.
It pops up with a grin,
Bread all toasted, let's begin!

In this space of playful fun,
Every heartbeat is a pun.
From silly hats to wiggly worms,
Endless laughter, my heart churns!

So with a twist and a bend,
Life's oddities never end.
With each step taken here,
Tomorrow laughs, it's crystal clear!

Passage of Hidden Secrets

In the closet, socks parade,
A secret world that's made.
Tangled up in yarn and fluff,
Do we really have enough?

Behind a curtain, lost and found,
An old hat rests on the ground.
Whispers of socks that stole the show,
In this room, anything can flow!

At the back of the garage,
A treasure chest perhaps a mirage.
Dust bunnies dance with broken toys,
Creating ruckus, just for noise!

A magic wand or maybe just a broom,
In every corner, giggles loom.
Secrets held in boxes of cheer,
Each adventure starts here, oh dear!

Opening to the Unseen

Peeking through an old keyhole,
I spy an enormous troll.
He's wearing socks upon his head,
And can't remember where he's led.

With a laugh that shakes the ground,
He breathes out clouds—oh, what a sound!
Behind him lies a hidden spree,
Mysteries unravel like a cup of tea!

A jiggle here, a jump over there,
What's that buzzing in the air?
A universe of giggles and shouts,
Where every shadow dances about!

Through this space of silly sights,
Life's too short for boring nights.
So open wide, let it be seen,
A world bursts forth, oh what a scene!

Threshold of Change

Just beyond the seasoned frame,
Lies a world that's never the same.
With gumdrops hanging from the tree,
It's a change nobody could foresee!

Walking through with shoes on tight,
I trip on giggles, what a sight!
With every step, the ground gives way,
Dancing shoes come out to play!

A plush unicorn plays the trombone,
Announcing all that's newly grown.
From jelly beans sprouting on the grass,
Who knew change could come to pass?

So let's embrace the quirks and spins,
With grins that swallow our chagrins.
On this threshold, fun's the aim,
In the land of laughter, no one's the same!

Portal of New Beginnings

Knock, knock, it's time to play,
A portal greets the everyday.
With a quack, a jump, a silly spin,
Who knew such fun could begin?

A squirrel winks, offers a nut,
Watch your step, or you might strut.
Through the arch, with glee unbound,
You'll find laughter all around.

Chickens dance in polka dots,
While cows skate on noodle lots.
Jump in boots, make a splash,
In this world, you'll surely dash.

So grab a hat, put on a smile,
Take a ticket for this wild mile.
Adventure waits, come take a peek,
At silly magic, so unique!

The Unlatched Invitation

There's a mailbox with a grin,
Squeaking open, jump right in!
Flip a coin, toss a shoe,
Guest list waits, just for you.

A giraffe with a party hat,
Says, "Come join, just make a splat!"
Balloons bouncing, skates in sight,
In this place, it feels just right.

Chickens juggle, pigs do flips,
Who knew socks could sprout such quips?
A cake that sings a birthday tune,
Dance along beneath the moon.

So don your best, and don't be late,
For laughter's flowing, check your fate!
With just a grin, your worries cease,
In this realm, it's purest peace!

Passage to Hidden Dreams

A passageway with glowing lights,
Leads to dreams that tickle tights.
Cactus plants in roller shoes,
Play charades with wacky cues.

Owls in shades sing easily,
While fish hold court with glee!
Beneath the stars that swirl and sway,
Join the fun, don't run away!

Flying pies and dancing beans,
Jellyfish with silver sheens.
Grab a partner, do the twist,
In this passage, you can't resist!

So hop on pillows, bounce around,
Find the joy, it's all profound.
With every step, bring forth your song,
In this place, you can't go wrong!

Veil of Infinite Journeys

A veil of laughter, bright and bold,
Whispers tales once never told.
Moonbeams dance, tickles abound,
In this journey, joy is found.

Marshmallow clouds float on by,
Sipping lemonade from the sky.
Frogs on stilts are gathering round,
Hopping high with joyous sound.

A cat in boots, a dog on skis,
Join the fun with clever ease.
With every twist and every turn,
More adventures for us to learn.

So flutter through this woven space,
With giggles lighting every face.
In the veil, the world unfolds,
Infinite journeys, laughter molds.

Entryway of the Soul

There's a hallway so wide, with shoes everywhere,
Puppy socks, flip-flops, and even a bear.
I thought I'd find wisdom, or some secret tool,
But I tripped on a sneaker, oh what a fool!

Walls decorated with pictures, all mismatched,
One with a cat, and another, a hat.
A sign up above says, 'Welcome to the show!'
Am I in a gallery or a circus down low?

The ceiling hangs low, made of woolly string,
I swear it's a place where sock puppets sing.
A squeaky old floorboards, they creak and they moan,
Each step feels like dancing on someone's old phone.

But if laughter's the treasure, this place is a gold,
With quirks and oddities, a sight to behold.
I'll stay here forever, and maybe forget,
That wisdom's the goal, but humor's the best bet.

Crossing to Another Place

There's a bridge made of jelly, sticky and bright,
If you cross it carefully, watch for mid-flight!
The paths are all wobbly, like funhouse floors,
You'll bounce and you'll giggle, escape from the bore.

On the other side lies a land full of snacks,
Chocolate rivers and hills with potato chip backs.
So if you feel hungry, just hop on this route,
But the gummy bears chase you; oh what a hoot!

A sign at the end says, 'Adventure awaits,'
With a map drawn in crayon and candy cane gates.
Just don't take too long, or the sweet may dissolve,
Leave room for the laughter; that's how you evolve!

But watch out for squirrels, they're plotting a scheme,
To steal all your goodies and mess with your dream.
Crossing to another place, with nothing but cheer,
Remember to smile, it's the best souvenir!

Arch of Unfulfilled Wishes

Under an arch that's made out of wishes,
I tossed in a coin, and oh, how it swishes!
A wish for a chicken who dances on three,
Instead I got one that just giggles at me.

The stars twinkled brightly, I bought a few hopes,
An umbrella full of rainbows and oodles of soaps.
But when the wish came, it slipped through my hands,
Instead, I received a sock that just stands!

I tossed in an idea, so grand and so bold,
A fairy appeared, but she just played with my gold.
"I wished for a meal that's delicious and hot,
Instead I got noodles, just stuck in a pot!"

But isn't it funny? These wishes ask more,
For laughter and joy are what we adore.
So as dreams flop and life goes for a spin,
I'll keep tossing wishes and accept the din!

The Keyhole of Curiosity

Peering through a keyhole, oh what a sight,
A garden of whispers, bathed in moonlight.
There's a cat wearing glasses, reading a book,
Behind him, a gnome with a very strange look.

The flowers are giggling, they dance in the breeze,
While toadstools wear hats, like some fancy tease.
I thought I'd find secrets, or maybe a spell,
But instead, a party, where no one can tell!

A unicorn's juggling; a feat very rare,
While squirrels in tuxedos are casting their flair.
The clock ticks backward, so time's all a guess,
In this wacky place, I must learn to regress!

So if you find a keyhole, take heed of the fun,
Adventure is waiting—just peek, little one!
With each twist and turn, of laughter and cheer,
The keyhole of curiosity brings joy ever near!

Archway to Dreams Unfurled

Step right through, oh what a sight,
A sandwich waits, in morning light.
Cats wear hats and dogs can sing,
In this place, it's a funny thing.

Turtles skate on rainbow lanes,
While squirrels drive tiny trains.
Upside-down trees, a giggling breeze,
Time melts like ice cream with such ease.

Jump on a cloud, take a quick spin,
In this realm, the fun won't thin.
The clock does a dance, oh what a show,
Let's hurry up, there's more to know.

So grab your hat and don't be late,
Adventures start, don't hesitate.
Laughs and giggles at every turn,
With every step, your heart will yearn.

Portal to the Infinite

In a whirlwind of color, with swirling light,
A pot of gold that's just out of sight.
Llamas in tuxedos, they juggle and play,
Let's jump right in, hip hip hooray!

Sneak in past chickens all donning a cape,
And dance with the bees in a floral shape.
Backwards is forward, inside out too,
Nothing is normal in this zany zoo.

A river of chocolate, a mountain of cheese,
You'll find giggles here, if you please.
Count the stars with a wink and a grin,
It's impossible to be sad, let's begin!

So whether you skip or you leap, or you crawl,
In this silly space, you can do it all.
With laughter like bubbles, you'll soon be afloat,
In a world where the whimsical dreams and gloat.

Frame of Destiny

Peepers peek through a pixelated screen,
What's on the other side? A jellybean machine!
Hula-hoops spin at an accelerating rate,
As potato chips dance on a giant plate.

Here, lemons wear glasses, they're reading a book,
While mice in pajamas decide how to cook.
Umbrellas parade in a fashion show,
And hammocks have dreams that they'd like to sow.

Follow the zebras, they've got a plan,
To lead you to cupcakes and a marching band.
A kazoo plays, and the cats tap their feet,
In this dreamy frame, time's utterly sweet.

So step on inside for a tickle and tease,
Every moment's a hoot, just do what you please.
Quack like a duck, or do a backflip,
In this playful frame, you won't want to skip!

The Uncommon Threshold

A penguin in slippers awaits your arrival,
With marshmallow chairs and a fun survival.
Join the party of frogs who sing out of tune,
As they waltz with the stars beneath the moon.

Balloons float by, each one a surprise,
A jester with glasses and googly eyes.
Magical jelly, that giggles with glee,
When you grab a spoon, then you'll see!

Riddles and puzzles float all around,
You'll chuckle and snort as you jump off the ground.
Time tickles your nose, it won't stand still,
As giggles escape, and you just can't chill.

So don your best hat, it's quite a strange show,
In this uncommon threshold, just let your heart glow.
Adventure awaits right around the bend,
So laugh and let playtime just never end!

Portal to the Unknown

A door swung wide with a creak,
Out popped a cat wearing a beak.
It meowed in rhymes, I could not see,
How it learned this from a talking tree.

In walked a penguin in high-heeled shoes,
Claiming it danced to disco blues.
"Join my conga!" it flapped a wing,
And suddenly, I couldn't do a thing!

A rabbit juggled jellybeans with flair,
In this odd place, nothing was rare.
A frog read poetry, dressed in a suit,
While I stood dumbfounded, failing to hoot.

So step right in if you want a laugh,
Just watch where you step, and don't be daft.
For every twist brings a surprising cheer,
Lurking right behind—your worst fear, my dear!

Entry to Infinite Realms

I found a gap that seemed quite large,
Expecting a wizard, maybe a barge.
Instead, a llama with shades and a hat,
Said, "Want to learn to chase after a rat?"

Next came a disco ball, spinning on air,
It twinkled its lights like it didn't care.
With funky moves and a loud clang,
The llama started dancing, making me fang.

Around the twist, a flying fish flew,
"Have you heard the news? I sing to you!"
It flopped and it flailed, but full of glee,
I couldn't help laughing, just being me.

And through this realm, the madness grew,
Unicorns burst in, wearing bright shade of blue.
So come along, and take my hand,
In this silly world, we'll make a grand stand!

Archway of Forgotten Whispers

An archway appeared in my backyard one day,
Whispers and giggles led me astray.
Behind it, a sock puppet played the lute,
Singing off-key, it didn't know how to hoot.

A gnome with a hat that towered up high,
Tried to sell me some candy made of pie.
I said, "What flavor?" He changed the plot,
"All of them! It's the best—come give it a shot!"

I went for a nibble; it tasted like cheese,
Mixed with marshmallows—oh, what a tease!
Then a smelly old troll popped up with a grin,
"You want my advice? Just jump right in!"

We danced through the whispers, round and round,
With each silly shimmy, more friends could be found.
If you chance upon something strange and bright,
Don't hide in confusion—join in the delight!

Frame of Unfolding Stories

In a frame that glows like a light bulb's spark,
A chicken recited the tales of the dark.
"Once I flew high, over valleys of green,
But ended up stuck in a marshmallow dream!"

By now, a tiny mouse wore a crown,
Gesturing grandly, it spun 'round and 'round.
"Stories unfold here, don't stay in your lane,
Join this mad circus—embrace all the strange!"

And just when I thought it couldn't get wilder,
A parrot in sneakers beatboxed, so riled up.
It echoed those tales with a twist and a spin,
Leaving me chuckling, feeling the grin.

So step into the frame, don't hold back your glee,
There's magic in laughter and endless spree.
Every tale told is a fabric of cheer,
In this wicked world—come, lend me your ear!

The Latch of Fate

A twist, a turn, oh what a sight,
My cat stuck in a box, tight!
With paws in air, it gives a yowl,
But every latch just makes me howl.

I fumble now, my hands all thumbs,
Chasing tails while making puns.
The latch clicks loud, a sound of cheer,
Out trotted my cat, with no fear.

A game of wits, this battle grand,
Who knew a box could take a stand?
The fate of fur, now turned around,
In all this chaos, joy is found.

So next time you feel stuck in place,
Remember laughter, warm embrace.
Just twist the latch and take a chance,
For life's a dance, not a circumstance.

The Unfolding Journey

A map unrolls, all creased and torn,
Where's the treasure? Oh, I'm worn!
Each fold a tale of places new,
Yet I'm lost in the middle, who knew?

With a compass spinning like a top,
I find myself at Mister Wop's shop.
He sells socks with lines and stripes,
In colors that cause raucous gripes.

A journey's fun when paths get crossed,
Like my shoe that's now embossed!
One foot in red, the other in blue,
A fashion statement, if you only knew.

So wander on with a silly grin,
Each turn's a laugh, a chance to win.
The journey unfolds, don't grab your maps,
For joy's in the mishaps, and hearty claps.

The Burgeoning Horizon

With every dawn, the sun peeks through,
A bird's eye view, the skies so blue.
Yet here I sit, with toast gone cold,
Dreams of journeys, I dare outright bold.

I painted wings but forgot to fly,
Now I'm stuck, yet oh so spry.
A cupcake here, a laugh with friends,
Life's playful chaos never ends.

Horizons shift and bend with time,
Like my favorite pair of socks, sublime!
They've holes and stains, but what a sight,
They dance with glee in morning light.

So lift your gaze and take a leap,
Where laughter grows, and joy runs deep.
In every rise, the horizon bends,
With silly stories that never ends.

Portal to the Past

A closet door, so worn and cracked,
What treasures lie? I'm quite unpacked.
Old shoes and coats, a royal mess,
Each item whispers tales of excess.

I slipped inside to find my youth,
A dance party with no set groove!
The music plays, my socks do sway,
Who knew past parties could come to play?

From polka dots to shiny gold,
My fashion sense was brave and bold.
But oh, what's this? A relic rare,
A wig from high school, with frizz and flair!

So journey back, embrace the grind,
In every trinket, joy you'll find.
The past is funny, alive with cheer,
A portal that brings laughter near.

Threshold to the Heart

In shoes untied, he takes a leap,
With a grin so wide, he doesn't peep.
Through a frame so squeaky, it's hard to tell,
If it's joy or chaos, such a funny spell.

A cat trots by, with a sassy glare,
As the welcome mat says, "Please don't share!"
He stumbles in, with arms so wide,
To hug the fridge, it's a foolish ride.

They say, in life, one must embrace,
Moments of laughter, a cheerful chase.
He winks at the walls that seem to chat,
"This is my kingdom, my humble habitat!"

Each corner hums, with a curious tune,
Dancing jigsaw puzzles, under the moon.
And as he spins, his socks take flight,
What a welcome sight, in the late night light!

Cracked Shell of the Ordinary

There's a crack in the plan, a twist in fate,
The smart fridge winks, can't be late!
A toddler rides a dog, what a sight,
In the realm of goofy, they all ignite.

Chairs are missing legs, books start to sing,
The cat joins in, oh the joy it brings!
Through mismatched socks and a lively chase,
Every moment favors a silly embrace.

But wait! A spider dons a tiny vest,
Hosting a dance, who'd have guessed?
With sandwiches marching in rows so neat,
Life finds a way to really compete.

The fish in the bowl wears a crown of seaweed,
Declaring himself the king of this breed.
As the oven giggles, it warms up the heat,
In this cracked shell, ordinary's sweet!

The Secret Knock

A knock-knock joke hidden in the wall,
With a secret knock, who would call?
The toaster pops up with a grin,
"Your breakfast awaits, where to begin?"

The dog's tail wags in rhythm and cheer,
As he whispers softly, "Have no fear!"
The fridge is a bard, spinning tales of old,
Of cakes and pies, both jiggly and bold.

Shadowy corners filled with bright ideas,
Like frogs in tuxedos, with tiny cheers.
A tap-tap-tap, and a muffled laugh,
What secrets are stored in this comical path?

A squirrel in a hat asks for a snack,
"Forget your diet, let's get off track!"
With each little thump, a surprise unfolds,
In the secret realm where laughter beholds!

Opening the Forgotten

A creak in the hinge sends shivers delight,
Whispers of chaos spring into sight.
An old toy robot, with a dazzling spin,
Laughs at the dust, and the fun can begin.

The forgotten hat sits, with feathers askew,
"Put me back on!" shouts the raccoon crew.
As marbles roll off in a playful spree,
All memories awaken for us to see.

An echo of laughter, a gleam in the night,
With socks doing tango, oh what a sight!
A lost shoe declares that it's time for a jig,
In the realm of the quirky, who needs a twig?

With every twist, and every clatter,
The past starts to feel like a sunny platter.
So come grab a snack, in this funny den,
For the forgotten turn up, and dance again!

Doorway of Forgotten Echoes

A creaky hinge sings a tune,
Of past laughter under the moon.
A sock appears, it's not alone,
The echo of shoes that no one's known.

Chasing shadows with a silly grin,
Who knew a hallway held such kin?
The laughter lingers, tickling the air,
As dust bunnies boogie without a care.

In slippers adorned with two left feet,
Each step is a dance, oh so sweet!
With echoes sneaking a cheeky peek,
Every corner shares a joke unique.

So tiptoe through this merry maze,
Where silliness reigns and banter plays.
The echoes beckon, come take a chance,
In this hallway of giggles, let's dance!

Passage into Whimsy

Through this corridor, so twisted and fun,
A merry-go-round with no end begun.
A hat flies past with a wink and a wink,
What awaits here is hard to think!

A cactus wearing a top hat tall,
Challenges you to a dance, after all.
Teacups swirling in laughter and cheer,
Spinning the tales of yonder year.

Beware the broom that has a mind,
It sweeps the floor but leaves words behind.
Tickling toes with each little twirl,
In this passage, let laughter unfurl.

So leap to joy at each playful nook,
Even the mirror can't help but look.
In this realm of whimsy, lost and found,
Be prepared for giggles to abound!

Gateway of Serendipity

A portal appears with steam and a flash,
It invites you in for a quirky bash.
A rubber chicken serenades the crowd,
With tunes so silly, they're laughter loud.

Penguins in tuxedos dance with flair,
While jellybeans rain down like fresh air.
Each corner reveals an odd delight,
Unexpected treasures, oh what a sight!

A calendar flipped to a random day,
Shows hoedowns with llamas in bright display.
They prance and they twirl, much like a spree,
In this serendipitous jamboree.

So step right in without a care,
Here, joy blooms anywhere, I swear!
Open your heart to sweet, silly fate,
And find yourself among giggles innate!

The Invitation to Wander

A signpost swings with a playful tone,
Whispers of paths not often known.
One says 'ice cream', another 'fuzzy',
In this world of whimsy, nothing's busy.

A raccoon in glasses leads with flair,
Through forests of candy, showcasing rare.
With every step, a ticklish surprise,
Funny creatures blink with mischief in their eyes.

A river of jelly flows swiftly by,
On marshmallow rafts, humans can fly.
With each giggle a bubble will burst,
In this invitation, joy's not rehearsed.

So grab a whimsical friend or two,
Join the merry wander, it's waiting for you!
In realms where laughter and fun intertwine,
Life becomes merrier, sweet, and divine!

Passage of Celestial Light

In the hallway, a ruckus begins,
A squirrel in a tie, spinning wins.
Chasing its tail, what a sight to behold,
It found a shoe, thinking it gold.

A wink from a lamp, as it wobbles about,
Bouncing to music, no need to shout.
Twinkling and clapping, the ceiling fan sways,
While the cat plans a coup for the rest of the days.

The mirror giggles, reflecting the scene,
As the squirrel pirouettes, feeling quite keen.
Who knew a shoe could unleash such delight?
This passage of light brings joy day and night.

So step right through, join the playful spree,
You might trip on a rabbit or dance with a bee.
With chortles of laughter echoing wide,
In this corridor where the silly abide.

Gateway to Rediscovery

Open wide for a curious quest,
Where socks become unicorns, that's the best!
A fridge with secrets, no one shall know,
Why the pickles are dancing to a disco show.

A pot of old plants claiming to be sage,
Advising the toaster on the latest page.
With crumbs acting as wise, tiny old men,
They tut at the chaos, then start it again.

The couch is a ship, sailing toward snacks,
With pillows as crew, all wearing bright hats.
Every creak in the floor adds a note to the song,
In this gateway where you truly belong.

So let your heart wander, feel free to roam,
Rediscover the magic that calls you back home.
With giggles and hiccups, joy unconfined,
In the silliness found, a treasure you'll find.

Edge of Uncharted Territory

At the edge of the room, a dance begins,
Where little green monsters wear silly grins.
Juggling spaghetti, under the old chair,
Beware of my cat, who's plotting a scare!

The shadows are whispering tales of delight,
While lost socks are plotting a daring flight.
An umbrella thinks it's a hat for the night,
And the vacuum pretends to take off in fright.

In the corner, odd socks hold a great ball,
With mismatched partners, they twirl and they sprawl.
The walls hold their laughter, wrapped tight like a gift,
On this unknown edge, let your spirit lift.

So venture on forth, dare to explore,
In this realm of nonsense, who could ask for more?
With giggles and wonders, oh what a spree,
At the edge of this land, just come dance with me!

Entryway to What Lies Beyond

A portal to chaos with each silly step,
Universe hiccups, I think it just wept.
Here comes a teddy, ready to ride,
On the back of a llama, oh what a glide!

The rug holds a party, snacks galore,
While a snail plays piano, it's never a bore.
With juice from the fridge doing backflips in cheer,
Every moment aflame, with laughter so dear.

In this entryway, time does a twist,
A banana in sunglasses steals every list.
Post-it notes dance, tuning in to the beat,
Together they wiggle, swaying their feet.

So open your heart to this riotous spree,
With whimsy and wonder, just come laugh with me.
In this bizarre place, joy knows no bounds,
Through the twists and the turns, pure fun abounds!

Passage of Time's Embrace

In the hallway, I stand and stare,
Wondering if socks have a pair.
Time's tickling laughs echo near,
While my lunch grows cold, oh dear!

A clock's a joker, spinning its hand,
Saying, "Hurry up!" while I just stand.
The sandwich yells, "Eat me, please!"
But I'm lost in the tickle of time's tease.

My shoes are dancing, ready to go,
But I'm stuck in the world of who knows?
Tick-tock tickles paint the scene,
As I ponder if I should've eaten green.

Time's a clown wearing oversized shoes,
Teasing me as I ponder my dues.
When finally I'm ready to explore,
I trip on my laces and roll on the floor!

Frame of Infinite Potential

In a little box, dreams come to play,
They giggle and dance, then run away.
A vast universe in a tiny frame,
Yet here I am, feeling quite lame.

I shake the frame, hoping they'd stay,
But they pop like bubbles, far from the fray.
One whispers, "Try to catch me, dude!"
While I'm stuck 'til four, quite in the mood.

Oh, the pictures that dance on the wall,
Each one promising a wild ball.
"Come join us!" they laugh and shout,
As I wrangle my lunch, full of doubt.

With every click of my camera, a chance,
To capture a giggle in a silly dance.
Yet instead, I capture a sneeze,
And now my friends are rolling in the breeze!

Threshold of Possibilities

At the edge of a world filled with glee,
I ponder just how fun it could be.
A step into it brings silly looks,
Like overcooked pasta and misplaced books.

The grass is tickling my bare feet,
Bouncing around to a whimsical beat.
The sun gives a wink, clouds swirl and play,
While squirrels conduct the grand ballet.

What if the sky could taste like pie?
Or take a leap and learn to fly?
Holding candy canes on a feathered boat,
With jellybeans singing, 'Just stay afloat!'

Oh, possibilities, both grape and pear,
Make me giggle without any care.
With each wobbly step into the place,
I find that laughs wear the silliest face!

Gateway to Unseen Realms

A portal glimmers in the moonlight,
Where odd socks gather for a fright.
They whisper secrets, giggles on high,
Of realms where noodles dance in the sky.

In this world, jellybeans ride atop,
Rainbows that sparkle, never to stop.
Unicorns juggling while riding a cat,
Who's trying to figure where his hat's at?

With a hop and a skip, I step on through,
And suddenly my coffee says, "Boo!"
It's a party of snacks, a wild delight,
Where pickles wear glasses and disco all night.

The realms unseen are quite the sight,
Where all things awkward come to unite.
So I dance with my bagel, slip on a twist,
In this funny place, nothing's amiss!

Culmination of Changed Directions

One day I tripped on my shoelace,
Tumbling down just like a bear,
Found myself in a pasta place,
With spaghetti flying everywhere!

I asked the chef for some advice,
He served a plate that made me grin,
He said, "Life's too short for just plain rice!"
So now I'm stuck in carb-filled sin.

My friends all laugh, they say, 'Oh dear!'
'You've really lost your sense of style,'
But I'm the best-dressed man right here,
In my sauce-stained shirt, I'll stay awhile!

So here's a toast to odd detours,
For laughter lives in silly ways,
Embrace the wacky, loosen those lures,
And let the giggles fill your days!

Arch of New Beginnings

I wandered through a park one day,
And found a tree with eyes that winked,
It said, 'Hello, come out and play!'
So I sat down and sadly blinked.

Around the roots, a rabbit danced,
Wearing slippers and a top hat too,
It said, 'Let's take a silly chance!'
I laughed so hard, my face turned blue.

We played hopscotch on the breeze,
And skipped through puddles, oh so grand,
The world became a game with ease,
With every step, we took a stand.

So when the path seems odd and strange,
Just follow where the giggles lead,
For life is full of joyful change,
And laughter is the heart's true seed.

Entrance to Untamed Imagination

I knocked on walls of cotton candy,
And found a shop that sold me dreams,
Where unicorns danced with marzipan,
And rivers flowed in chocolate streams.

A sign proclaimed, 'No hugs allowed!'
But I defied the rule with glee,
I squeezed a giant, sticky cloud,
Which dripped and stuck right onto me!

I crafted hats from licorice,
And wore them like a king of jest,
In this wild world's sweet malice,
I found the joy of silly quests.

So wander forth with open mind,
To places filled with giggles and grins,
For every whimsy you will find,
Is where your greatest fun begins!

A Portal Called Hope

I found a mailbox on the street,
That whispered secrets in my ear,
It said, 'Drop in your wish, sweet treat!'
So I tossed in my fears and beer.

Out came a cat that spoke in rhymes,
With sparkly shoes and a cap that shone,
It grabbed my hand, said, 'Let's make times!'
We pranced around like we were alone.

We chased the squirrels, played peekaboo,
The trees were clapping with delight,
"Here comes the best of funky crew!"
They cheered us on, day turned to night.

So grab that dream that feels too wild,
And laugh at all the quirky jibes,
For every heart needs hope, like a child,
And joy is found in wild high-fives!

The Journey Within

In socks of mismatched hue, they stroll,
Through dreams of cookies, time takes its toll.
A cat in a hat gives advice so wise,
While giggles erupt under starry skies.

They twist like pretzels with silly grins,
After dodging the garden of runaway twins.
Chasing rainbows and ice cream trucks,
Finding magic in the world of clucks.

Each step a stumble on this goofy quest,
With shadows that dance in a wild jest.
Laughter bubbling like soda pop,
While washing the worries, they never stop.

They leap through puddles of laughter so bright,
With silly hats on, oh what a sight!
In this merry jaunt where oddities reign,
Life's a circus, just drop the mundane!

Portal of Awakening

A portal of feathers and jiggly tails,
Opens to land where laughter prevails.
Balloons that giggle and ticklish trees,
Invite all the folks to come down on their knees.

With shoes that honk and hats that squeak,
The antics unfold rather unique.
Breakfast foods doing the chicken dance,
Why not join in? Give it a chance!

A rabbit in slippers jumps on the scene,
With jokes in a pocket – what a routine!
The sunset splashes paint on silly frowns,
As moonbeams twirl in giggly gowns.

Through this passage of whimsy and cheer,
Every smile is sweeter with friends gathered near.
In the realm of zany, no worries allowed,
Come frolic and play in a merry crowd!

The Tapestry of Beginnings

Threads of laughter weave a bright tale,
As unicorns groan and fairies set sail.
An octopus cooking spaghetti for lunch,
With each tangled noodle, there's always a crunch.

The sun dances clumsily, tripping on rays,
While squirrels debate on the best nutty ways.
Giggling trees whisper secrets so sweet,
That snowflakes join in with their own little beat.

Each stitch a story, a twist in the plot,
Jellybeans bouncing – oh, what a thought!
Kites made of pancakes soar high in the sky,
Where giggles erupt and the silly birds fly.

In this fabric of fun, new dreams take flight,
Where jester hats twirl in the warm, sunny light.
Creating beginnings that twinkle and shine,
Every moment a joke, perfectly divine!

Passage to Unwritten Chapters

A wild ride awaits on this laughing ship,
With walruses giggling, can you take a dip?
Unwritten tales dance in the breeze,
As we munch on candy with whimsical ease.

The compass spins wildly, directions confuse,
As jellyfish guide us in sparkly shoes.
With waves of chuckles crashing ashore,
We treasure each moment, crave silly more.

Each chapter unwinds like a silly string,
While playful dolphins do their own swing.
A chorus of bananas as the prize we seek,
In this humorous journey, it's laughter we speak.

So open your heart to the unknown delight,
Each turn brings a giggle, each moment feels right.
In this passage of humor, let's dance and unfold,
For stories worth telling are treasures of gold!

Passage Through the Quiet

In a hallway filled with shoes,
I tripped on one, it gave me blues.
With a grunt and a wiggle, I slipped and slid,
And crashed through the wall like a cheeky kid.

Out I popped in a room of glee,
Where cats played chess and drank sweet tea.
A parrot squawked, 'Hey, what's the fuss?'
I shrugged and said, 'Well, it's all a plus!'

Next, I strolled to a scene bizarre,
Dancing llamas played guitar.
They wore sunglasses, strumming away,
Oh, what a wild unexpected day!

With every laugh and silly sight,
I found my worries took to flight.
So if you stumble, don't you fear,
Adventure waits just round the sphere!

Entry to the Unexpected

I pushed on a wall, not thinking twice,
Out popped a gnome, oh my, how nice!
He grinned and said, 'This door's a trick,
Step in the fun, it's all real quick.'

Then I fell into a rainbow slide,
Zooming fast with butterflies at my side.
They winked and giggled, flew all around,
In this zany place, there was joy unbound.

Next, I landed in a pool of jam,
Bouncing like a crazy spam can!
Grapes in googles were doing a swim,
I couldn't help but laugh on a whim!

An octopus with a chef's hat waved,
'Let's make some toast,' he eagerly braved.
With jellyfish flinging toasts in the air,
I knew right then, 'This life's beyond compare!'

Gateway of Time's Secrets

I opened a closet filled with shoes,
And out popped a T-Rex, spreading the news.
He danced with flair and a giant grin,
'Let's party hard, just jump right in!'

Through a swirl of colors, we zoomed along,
Past flying fish that sang a song.
On a clock's hand, a hippo skated,
Each tick-tock made the magic elevated.

I suddenly found myself in a shop,
Where socks and spoons would hop and bop.
A raccoon chef flipped pancakes high,
While kangaroos bounced beneath the sky!

With a flick of a whisk and a dash of flair,
The time flew by with a whoosh of air.
So if you see a strange closet bright,
Step inside, it might just feel right!

The Aperture of Adventure

A crack in the wall led me astray,
Into a circus where llamas play.
They wore big hats and juggled pies,
With popcorn popping before my eyes.

I wandered past a giant pink cat,
Who offered me a sparkling spat!
'Put it on, it'll make you dance,'
And soon enough, I took my chance!

Round and round the cotton candy haze,
I spun and twirled in a sugary daze.
An octopus wore roller skates,
As he'd glide by with carefree fates!

Out came a bear with a friendly grin,
Said, 'Join the fun, let the show begin!'
With laughter and joy filling the space,
In this wild world, I found my place!

Crossroads of Change

At the fork in the road, I tripped on a shoe,
The map said 'left', but clearly, it's askew.
A sign read 'future', but it looked like a truck,
Do I go with the flow or just risk my luck?

A chicken crossed over, I asked, 'Where's your aim?'
'Just winging it here, but it's all a game!'
The trees whispered secrets, the wind gave a laugh,
Change can be funny, and so is my path!

My GPS glitched, said 'you've reached your fate,'
I saw only squirrels, all gathered to mate.
A rabbit hopped by with a wink and a grin,
I'd follow his lead—where do I begin?

So here at the crossroads, I dance with delight,
With hiccups and chuckles, I'll soar like a kite.
Each twist and turn writes a hilarious tale,
Change isn't scary when you've got a good gale!

Beyond the Lattice

Peering through lattice, I saw a fine sight,
A cat in a top hat, oh what pure delight!
He tipped me a wink, then he juggled some fish,
'Come closer, dear friend, for a magical wish!'

Beyond the wood frame, the garden did sway,
A gnome rode a turtle, what a curious play!
They danced with the daisies, all dressed up in style,
I laughed at their antics, it could last a while.

'Why sit in the safe when the world is a stage?',
Cried the squirrel on stilts with a laugh on his page.
I pushed through the lattice, now ready for fun,
With laughter as fuel, and joy as my sun.

So here's to the moments where silliness thrives,
When laughter captures all of our drives.
With friends like the gnome and the dancing cat too,
Life's just a joke, and I'm humor's debut!

The Unseen Invite

An envelope came, with stickers and flair,
'You're invited!' it said, but I checked—wasn't there?
No address, no stamp, just a doddle of ink,
Was it real, or just something I'd dreamt in a blink?

I peeked through my curtains, the street was a mess,
Just my neighbor in pajamas, looking quite stressed.
He waved with a donut, had a party of one,
I guess I'll go join him; let's see how we run!

With confetti on dogs and a pinata of cheese,
The fun was unplanned, yet it brought me to ease.
We danced with the shadows and sang silly tunes,
Every laugh echoed, just like the cartoons.

So heed the unseen; joy's very sly,
Sometimes it's wrapped up in a napkin nearby.
With laughter as our host, and friends on the scene,
We'll celebrate whimsy, in ways unforeseen!

Portal of Collective Yearnings

In a quest for the snacks, I found a bright door,
With a silly sign: 'Get your wishes galore!'
I nudged it wide open, and what did I see?
A parade of llamas, all bellowing glee!

They danced on their hooves, wearing socks for their paws,
Each strut of their legs, an applause with a pause.
'We wish for more snacks!' said they in a cheer,
'And for humans who'll join us; we hold you quite dear!'

On wings of imagination, we floated as one,
Eating peanuts and popcorn, oh what silly fun!
A juggler was there with some fruit on his head,
He slipped and fell back into a pile of bread!

So step through the portal, embrace all the quirks,
In the realm of desires, jump around like jerks!
For laughter and snacks are the keys to the bliss,
In a circus of dreams, you don't want to miss!

The Secret of the Unseen

A tiny latch on a cliffside wall,
Leads to a mystery; who knows, could be small?
I peek with suspicion, my heart starts to race,
Is it a wormhole or just empty space?

My cat gives a meow, as if to suggest,
That maybe beyond there, I'll find a jest.
With one little push, and a glance at the floor,
I tumble right in, to a land made of kites galore!

In this realm of balloons, all wearing a hat,
The bushes are jellybeans, how 'bout that!
I dance with the trees, they giggle and shake,
It's a comical world, for goodness' sake!

So if you find a latch on the way to your home,
Give it a tug, my dear friend, and roam!
For laughter awaits where the wild things prance,
In the secret of unseen, join the fun and dance!

Crossover into the Unknown

With a step that feels silly, I slide on the floor,
To a place where I'll giggle, I want nothing more.
A flick of my wrist, and a chuckle escapes,
There's a realm of odd socks and talking grapes!

I met a wise owl, who shared a good pun,
'Why did the chicken? Oh wait, it's not done!'
In this nutshell of nonsense, my worries unwind,
As I sip on some lemonade with a twist of lime.

The sun throws confetti, the clouds wear a frown,
As I bounce with a penguin in a bright red gown.
"Join me for tea!" he says with a laugh,
His teapot's a teacup, oh what a gaffe!

So step off the ledge, embrace the absurd,
Cross into the unknown, let your joy be heard!
With each quirky turn, in this land of glee,
Find humor in wonders, just let yourself be!

The Charmed Opening

There stands a weird cupboard with a lock and a key,
Curiosity bubbles inside of me.
I twist it a bit, and what do I find?
A parade of bananas, all dancing in line!

The musicians are squirrels, they play with such flair,
Each note draws a giggle from the soft, comfy air.
With hats made of radishes, they strut and they spin,
I can't help but chuckle; let's join in the din!

They beckon me closer, "Come dance with the crew!"
So I waddle along, feeling quite like a fool.
With my arms like spaghetti and feet like a flap,
I join in the fun, in this momentous clap!

So when you see a charmer with a curious twist,
Don't hesitate now; you might just be missed!
With laughter as currency, join in like a pro,
You'll find a bright world in the charming tableau!

Threshold of Reflection

A quirky old mirror, all dusty and dim,
I glance at my reflection, half full, half thin.
But wait, as I squint, it starts to get fun,
My mirror self dances, oh look at that run!

I mimic her moves, and we both strike a pose,
Her hair is a hurricane; mine just a rose.
Together we twirl, cracking up at the sight,
A dance-off with Glee, oh what pure delight!

She sticks out her tongue, and you won't believe,
A rainbow erupts, making boredom just leave.
Suddenly, she gestures, "Let's jump to the side!"
And we tumble right through, on an absurd joyride!

With laughter ricocheting in this mirror realm's sheen,
The threshold to fun is alive and serene.
So if you find a mirror, just give it a wink,
And who knows what magic might be on the brink!

www.ingramcontent.com/pod-product-compliance
Lightning Source LLC
Chambersburg PA
CBHW060137230426
43661CB00003B/461